David Thompson

Momotaro

David Thompson

Momotaro

ISBN/EAN: 9783744704205

Printed in Europe, USA, Canada, Australia, Japan

Cover: Foto ©Thomas Meinert / pixelio.de

More available books at **www.hansebooks.com**

Japanese Fairy Tale Series, No. 1.

MOMOTARO.

(SECOND EDITION.)

PUBLISHED BY

KOBUNSHA,

2. Minami Saegicho.

TOKYO.

日本昔噺第一號

米國 ダビッド タムソン 譯述

再版 桃太郎

鮮齋永濯畫

明治十八年八月十七日版權免

許同年九月出版同十九年八

月廿六日再版幷添題御屆

東京麴區南佐柄木町二番地

出版所 弘文社

MOMOTARO

or

Little Peachling.

A long long time ago there lived an old man and an old woman. One day the old man went to the mountains to cut grass; and the old woman

went to the river to wash clothes.
While she was washing a great
big thing came tumbling and
splashing down the stream.
When the old woman saw it

she was very glad, and pulled
it to her with a piece of bam-
boo that lay near by. When
she took it up
and looked at it

she saw that it was a very large peach. She then quickly finished her washing and returned home intending to give the peach to her old man to eat.

When she cut the peach in two, out came a child from the large kernel. Seeing this the old couple rejoiced, and named the child Momotaro, or Little Peachling, because he came out of a peach. As both the old people took good care of him, he grew and became strong and enterprising. So the old couple had their expectations raised, **and** bestowed still more care **on** his education.

Momotaro finding that he excelled every body in strength determined to cross over to the island of the devils, take their riches, and come back. He at once consulted with the old man and

the old woman about
the matter, and got them to
make him some dumplings.
These he put in his pouch.
Besides this he made every
kind of preparation for his
journey to the island of the
devils and set out.

Then first a dog came to
the side of the way and said;

"Momotaro! What have you there hanging at your belt?" He replied: "I have some of the very best Japanese millet dumplings." "Give me one and I will go with you," said the dog. So Momotaro took a dumpling out of his pouch and gave it to the dog. Then a monkey came and got one the same way. A pheasant also came flying and said: "Give me a dumpling too, and I will go along with you." So all three went along with him. In no time they arrived at the island of the devils, and at once broke through the front gate; Momotaro first; then his three followers. Here they met a great multitude of the devil's retainers who showed fight, but

they pressed still inwards, and at last encountered the chief of the devils, called Akandoji. Then came the tug of war. Akandoji made at Momotaro with an iron club, but Momotaro was ready for him, and dodged him adroitly.

At last they grappled each other, and without difficulty Momotaro just crushed down Akandoji and tied him with a rope so tight that he could not even move. All this was done in a fair fight.

After this Akandoji the chief of the devils said he would surrender all his riches. "Out with your riches then:" said Momotaro laughing. Having collected and ranged in order a great pile of precious things, Momotaro took them, and set out for his home, rejoicing, as he marched bravely back, that,

with the help of his three companions, to whom he attributed all his success, he had been able so easily to accomplish his end.

Great was the joy of the old man and the old woman when Momotaro came back. He feasted every body bountifully, told many stories of his

adventure, displayed his riches,
and at last became a leading man,
a man of influence, very rich and
honorable; a man to be very much
congratulated indeed!!

The Kobunsha's Japanese Fairy Tale Series.

Published by the KOBUNSHA, 2, Minami Saegicho, TOKYO